FUNGI

****

THE KINGDOMS OF LIFE

FUNGI

* * * * * * * * * * * * * * * *

DR. ALVIN, VIRGINIA, AND ROBERT SILVERSTEIN

TWENTY-FIRST CENTURY BOOKS

* *

A Division of Henry Holt and Company

New York

MAY 'υ (1 1997

Twenty-First Century Books
A Division of Henry Holt and Company, Inc.
115 West 18th Street
New York, NY 10011

Henry Holt® and colophon are trademarks of
Henry Holt and Company, Inc.
Publishers since 1866

Published in Canada by Fitzhenry & Whiteside Ltd.
195 Allstate Parkway, Markham, Ontario L3R 4T8

Library of Congress Cataloging-in-Publication Data
Silverstein, Alvin.
Fungi / Alvin Silverstein, Virginia Silverstein, and Robert Silverstein.—1st ed.
p   cm.—(The Kingdoms of life)
Summary: Introduces fungi, discussing their varieties, physical structure,
reproduction, role in the ecosystem, and uses.
Includes index.
1. Fungi—Juvenile literature. [1. Fungi.] I. Silverstein, Virginia B. II. Silverstein, Robert A.
III. Title. IV. Series: Silverstein, Alvin. The Kingdoms of life.
QK603.5.S54   1996
589.2—dc20   95–42326
                                                                                CIP
                                                                                AC

ISBN 0–8050–3520–6
First Edition 1996

Designed by Kelly Soong

Printed in the United States of America
All first editions are printed on acid-free paper ∞.
10 9 8 7 6 5 4 3 2 1

Photo credits

Cover: Jeff Lepore/Photo Researchers, Inc.
p. 6 (clockwise from top right): Dave B. Fleetham/Tom Stack & Associates; Rod Planck/Tom Stack & Associates; Cabisco/Visuals Unlimited; M. I. Walker/Photo Researchers, Inc.; Zig Leszczynski/Earth Scenes; Bill Gause/Photo Researchers, Inc.; pp. 7, 38 (middle): Rod Planck/Tom Stack & Associates; pp. 8, 16: Doug Wechsler/Earth Scenes; p. 9: Photo Researchers, Inc.; p. 10 (left): F. E. Unverhau, FPSA/Earth Scenes; p; 10 (right): E. R. Degginger/Earth Scenes; p. 13: Stanley Flegler/Visuals Unlimited; p. 14: G. I. Bernard/Earth Scenes; pp. 19, 25 (left): John Shaw/Tom Stack & Associates; p. 20 (clockwise from top): G. Shih & R. Kessel/Visuals Unlimited; G. Shih & R. Kessel/Visuals Unlimited; D. M. Phillips/Visuals Unlimited; D. M. Phillips/Visuals Unlimited; A. M. Siegelman/Visuals Unlimited; R. Calentine/Visuals Unlimited; p. 21: Michael Fogden/Earth Scenes; p. 24: James W. Richardson/Visuals Unlimited; pp. 25 (right), 38 (left & right), 43 (top): David M. Dennis/Tom Stack & Associates; p. 27: Dr. Nigel Smith/Earth Scenes; p. 28 (top): W. E. Fry/Visuals Unlimited; p. 28 (bottom): Jack M. Bostrack/Visuals Unlimited; p. 31 (top): Zig Leszcznski/Earth Scenes; pp. 31 (bottom), 48, 54 (bottom): Cabisco/Visuals Unlimited; pp. 32, 33, 47 (right): John D. Cunningham/Visuals Unlimited; p. 35: J. N. Reichell/Photo Researchers, Inc.; p. 37: V. A. Wilmot/Visuals Unlimited; p. 39: Milton Rand/Tom Stack & Associates; p. 40: Kerry T. Givens/Tom Stack & Associates; p. 41 (left): G. A. Maclean/Earth Scenes; p. 41 (middle): Dale J. Sarver/Earth Scenes; p. 41 (right): Michael P. Gadmoski/Earth Scenes; p. 43 (bottom): Jack Wilburn/Earth Scenes; p. 47 (left): G. Shih & R. Kessel/Visuals Unlimited; p. 50: John Eastcott & Yva Momatiuk/Earth Scenes; p. 52 (upper left): Doug Sokell/Tom Stack & Associates; p. 52 (upper right & bottom): Gerald & Buff Corsi/Tom Stack & Associates; p. 54 (top): R. F. Ashley/Visuals Unlimited; p. 55: Milton H. Tierney, Jr./Visuals Unlimited.

CONTENTS

* * * * * * * *

THE KINGDOMS OF LIFE

ANIMALS

Great horned owl

VERTEBRATES

Day octopus

INVERTEBRATES

PLANTS

Silver vase

FUNGI

Hygrophorus mushroom

MONERANS

Cyanobacteria

PROTISTS

Diatoms

FUNGI

1

****

OUR LIVING WORLD

****

YOU USE CLASSIFICATION EVERY DAY

You use classification when you go shopping at the supermarket. The grocer has placed thousands of different grocery items on the shelves in an orderly way, by placing similar objects in related groups. Imagine if you had to sort through cans of baked beans, fresh-baked rolls, salami, oranges, soft drinks, ice-cream sandwiches, and dozens of other foods when all you wanted was a carton of milk! Because the goods in the supermarket are sorted into groups, you can find what you want easily by going to its particular section. Fresh fruits and vegetables are in their own section, breakfast cereals are all together, and so are dairy products, juices, and canned soups.

Like items are grouped in a market to make them easier to find. This is one type of classification system.

Scientists have observed and described nearly two million different kinds of living things. But no one knows how many kinds there really are on earth, or how many have become extinct. Each year 7,000 to 10,000 new species are identified and named, and each day about 100 species are lost!

Imagine trying to learn about that many creatures! How could you keep all their names straight, much less remember the important facts about them? One way would be to find patterns and relationships. Similar types of organisms could be grouped together and compared to other groups. Biologists have been doing just that for many centuries. Each new creature that is discovered is placed in the group that is the best match for it; it is classified.

Classification is the process of dividing objects into related groups. Taxonomy is the science of classifying or arranging living things into groups based on characteristics they share. It comes from the Greek words *taxis*, which means "arrangement," and *nomos*, which means "law."

LINNAEUS, THE FATHER OF TAXONOMY

The classification system used today is based on binomial nomenclature, a system devised by the eighteenth-century Swedish botanist and naturalist Carl Linnaeus. Each living thing is given a two-part name based on some of its most important characteristics. The first name corresponds to a genus, a group of rather closely related kinds of organisms. The second name, the species, identifies the particular kind of creature within the genus. For example, the destroying angel, *Amanita virosa*; the fly agaric mushroom, *Amanita muscaria*; and Caesar's mushroom, *Amanita caesarea*, all belong to the same genus, *Amanita*. They are related organisms that have many things in common, but they have enough differences to be considered as separate species. Knowing which is which can be very important to people who eat mushrooms! The destroying angel and fly agaric are poisonous, but the Caesar's mushroom has been considered a delicacy since the time of the ancient Romans.

Carl Linnaeus (1707–1778) devised the scientific method of naming living things. He wrote books in Latin on the classification of plants and animals.

Scientific names often describe a characteristic of an organism. In the destroying angel's scientific name, *Amanita virosa*, *virosa* comes from the Latin word for "poison." *Morchella esculenta* tells us that the mushroom with this name is good to eat. (*Esculenta* is Latin for "edible.") Sometimes a species is named after a person, like *Amanita caesarea* for the Roman emperor.

Linnaeus did more than just establish a two-name system for identifying related species. He outlined a larger framework into which all the living

Destroying angel (Amanita virosa)—***deadly!***

Caesar's mushroom (Amanita caesarea)—
delicious!

species could be placed according to their relationships to others. Related **genera** (the plural of **genus**) were classified in larger groups, called **families**. The members of a family share a number of characteristics in common, but not as many similarities as are found among the members of each genus within the family. The taxonomic families are grouped into still larger categories, called **orders**, and related orders, in turn, are grouped into **classes**. Those are part of larger groups called **phyla** (**phylum** is singular), and each phylum fits into one of the major **kingdoms** of life.

Each successive group in the classification system contains a smaller number of organisms, which are more closely related to one another. Phylum Basidiomycota, for example, contains large mushrooms and puffballs and also rusts and smuts, which cause plant diseases. Within this phylum, the class Homobasidiomycetes includes just mushrooms, puffballs, and other large fungi; the rusts and smuts belong to a different class, Heterobasidiomycetes.

MEMORY AIDS

* *

Silly sentences can help you remember lists. The first letters of

Keep **P**uffballs **C**ool **O**r **F**ind **G**ood **S**helter

can help you remember the major groups of the scientific classification system:

Kingdom, **P**hylum, **C**lass, **O**rder, **F**amily, **G**enus, **S**pecies.

(To help you remember, picture a hot puffball exploding!)

2
****
THERE'S A FUNGUS AMONG US
****

The explorers pressed deeper into the forest, searching for traces of the monstrous creature. Each time they found one, they carefully noted its position and snipped off specimens to take back to the lab. By the time they finished mapping the monster's domain, they calculated that its huge body covered an area of 2.5 square miles (4 square kilometers) and weighed nearly 1,000 tons!

This was not a scene from a science fiction thriller on TV. It really happened, right here on planet earth, in 1992. And the monster is still there, living and growing in the soil beneath a pine forest southeast of Seattle, Washington. Bigger than any blue whale or giant sequoia tree, it may be the largest creature that ever lived on earth. What is it? A humongous fungus!

WHAT IS A FUNGUS?

Have you ever eaten mushrooms? Have you ever found molds growing on leftovers that stayed in the refrigerator too long, or dark smudges of mildew on that damp towel you left in your gym locker? Have you ever baked bread and used yeast to make the dough rise? Mushrooms, molds, mildew, and yeast are all fungi. But what do they have in common, and how do they fit into the world of life on our planet?

In an ancient Arabian book, fungi were considered only half alive and were placed on the ladder of life somewhere between minerals and plants. Up to about the middle of this century, most scientists and other knowledgeable people would have said that fungi are plants. The world of life was divided into two major kingdoms, plants and animals. Fungi definitely weren't animals—they didn't move, and they didn't have eyes, ears, or other sense organs to perceive their environment, nor did they have any nerves or other means of coordinating their body activities. Yet they did grow and reproduce themselves as living things do. So they must be plants. But the plant kingdom wasn't a very good fit for fungi, either. Unlike most plants, they do not have the green chemical chlorophyll, and they do not make their own food. To survive, fungi have to take in food materials from the bodies of living or dead plants or animals. Fungi do not have roots, stems, leaves, flowers, or seeds, as most plants do. Unlike plants, fungi don't need light to live, so they can exist in dark places, such as underground caves, dark closets, and cellars.

Fungi are not the only creatures that do not fit very well into a two-kingdom scheme of life. Eventually most scientists decided that a better framework was needed to classify all of earth's life-forms. Now the most generally accepted division is a five-kingdom scheme, in which the major divisions are:

Mushroom farming is frequently done in caves because certain fungi grow best in the dark.

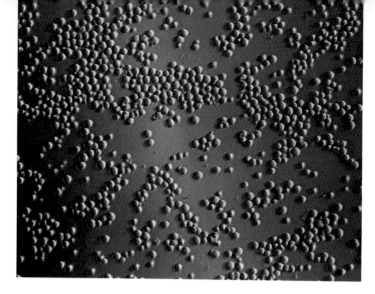

Microscopic yeast fungus (Saccharomyces cerevisiae) produces carbon dioxide from the carbohydrates in dough. The gas makes the dough rise.

Kingdom Monera (bacteria and other primitive single-celled forms)

Kingdom Protista (single-celled animal-like and plantlike forms, as well as some multicellular organisms closely related to them)

Kingdom Fungi (plantlike organisms that lack chlorophyll and do not make their own food)

Kingdom Plantae (true plants)

Kingdom Animalia (true animals)

AN UNDERAPPRECIATED KINGDOM

Most people have a rather negative opinion of the kingdom Fungi. Molds and mildews rot our food and make our cellars smell musty. They leave ugly spots around our bathtubs and on our shower curtains. Many people are allergic to their tiny microscopic spores (seedlike structures that grow into new fungi). Fungi cause athlete's foot and jock itch and make our sneakers smell stinky.

Fungi aren't all bad, though. Although there are a number of poisonous mushrooms, there are many types that a lot of people find delicious to eat. Fungi are used to make penicillin and other lifesaving drugs. Bread rises because of a microscopic fungus called yeast. Fungi are used to ripen and flavor some cheeses and to make soy sauce.

Fungi are important recyclers in nature, too. They break down dead animals and plants into simple compounds that are returned to the soil. This is called **decomposition**. Plants can use these compounds to grow. Fungi and bacteria are the main decomposers of organic matter on our planet. They are as important to the balance of nature as the food producers (plants and some bacteria). If dead plants and animals were not recycled, with their nutrients returned to the soil and water for other living things to use, they would pile up and cover the earth, and their chemicals could not be reused by new generations of life.

Fungi can be found almost everywhere—in the air, soil, and water. About 100,000 different kinds of fungi have been classified. The study of fungi is called **mycology**, and the scientists who study them are **mycologists**. (Mycology comes from the Greek words *mykes*, which means "mushroom," and *logos*, meaning "study.") Mycologists think that there are another 200,000 fungi waiting to be named.

ANCIENT FUNGI

Fungi first appeared on earth more than 350 million years ago, long before flowering plants. They are believed to have evolved from a type of single-celled organism that no longer exists today. Some kinds of fungi are now extinct, but others that existed hundreds of millions of years ago can still be found today.

HOME SWEET HOME FOR A FUNGUS

Some fungi can live in many different kinds of places (habitats). Others can live only in a specific habitat where the conditions are exactly right.

Many fungi can live in very hot or cold environments where other living things couldn't survive. Fungi have been found growing around the hot springs of volcanoes. Have you ever found a moldy orange in your refrigerator? Refrigerating food prevents bacteria from growing, but it won't prevent mold from growing on fruits and vegetables, or in a jar of jelly. Fungi can also live in places that are very salty or very sugary. Most other living things can't survive under those conditions. Many living things die when their surroundings become very dry, but quite a few fungi can change into a resting stage, which allows them to survive dry periods.

FUNGI LIFESTYLES

Fungi get their nourishment either from organic material, which was once part of a plant or animal—such as rotten wood, bread, cheese, and fruit—or from living things. Fungi that live on decaying materials are called **saprophytes**. Those that live on animals and plants are called **parasites**. (A parasite is an organism that takes its nourishment from the body of another organism without giving anything useful in return.) Parasitic fungi include chestnut blight, which has wiped out most of the chestnut trees in the United States, wheat rust, and potato blight. Other fungus parasites attack invertebrates and vertebrates, including the fungi that cause ringworm and athlete's foot in humans. Some fungi are parasites of other fungi. Fungi can even be parasites of microscopic creatures. A fungus called *Amoebaphilus* is just what its name means—an ameba lover!

Some fungi grow on only one type of food, such as dead leaves, tree stumps, dead grass, or animal manure. Other fungi can live on many different kinds of food. Some fungi can change their feeding habits when conditions change. Honey mushrooms (such as the humongous fungus in Washington State) normally live on dead stumps and branches. But occasionally they can produce thick, black, shoelacelike structures (**rhizomorphs**) that grow through the soil until they reach the roots of a live tree. Then the fungus spreads through the tree, eventually killing it.

A number of fungi live with plants but are not parasites. Each organism benefits

The honey mushroom (Armillaria mellea) *helps to decompose dead wood.*

from the other. The two organisms are said to have a **symbiotic relationship**. A **lichen** is formed when a fungus and an alga live symbiotically. The alga provides food, and the fungus prevents the lichen from drying out and attaches it to a surface. Many kinds of trees, shrubs, and herbs also form symbiotic relationships with fungi. The fungi live on the roots of these plants. The fungus supplies the plants with nitrogen and minerals, while obtaining moisture and carbohydrates from the plant. This symbiotic relationship is called a **mycorrhiza**.

3
****

FUNGI:
THE INSIDE STORY

****

Yeasts are simple single-celled organisms, but most fungi are many celled. The mushroom is the best known fungus. The body of a fungus is made up of thousands of fine, threadlike filaments called **hyphae** (**hypha** is the singular). The hyphae of some fungi are so thin that it would take 50,000 of them, laid side by side, to equal 1 inch (2.5 centimeters)! The rhizomorphs of fungi like the honey mushroom are bundles of hyphae, as much as 0.04 inch (1 millimeter) thick. These tough, cordlike strands allow the fungus to spread over places where there is no food or water. The outer hyphae have thicker, protective walls, while the inner hyphae carry water and food to the fungus while it spreads.

The cell wall of a fungus does not contain **cellulose,** the chemical that stiffens the cell walls of green plants. Instead, another carbohydrate, fungal **chitin,** gives it strength. (This is similar to the material that is found in the exoskeleton, or outer shell, of insects.)

The hyphae form a tangled mat or web of interweaving threads, called a **mycelium**, that grows in the substance on which the fungus is feeding. Growth occurs only from the tips of the hyphae. Fungi can't move, but a fungus can spread out and find new food sources when the mycelium grows. The mycelium can grow very quickly. If you took the hyphae that some fungi can grow in a single day and placed them end to end, they would stretch out more than a half-mile (one kilometer) in length. The mycelium of a fungus can be compared to the roots, stem, and leaves of a green plant.

If a piece of mycelium is broken off and carried to a new place, it may grow into a whole new fungus. This is one way that fungi reproduce. (Mushroom farmers use this method to grow new mushrooms.) But most fungi have another way to reproduce. Thousands of fungal filaments combine to form a **fruiting body**, such as the umbrella-

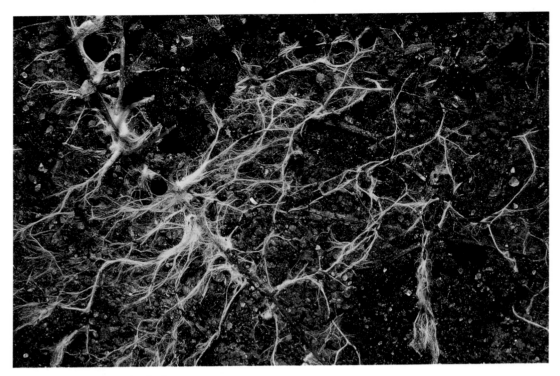

The mycelium network of a fungus

shaped part of a mushroom that we see sticking out of the ground. (Most of the organism, the mycelium, is found underground.)

The fruiting body is like the fruit of a plant. **Spores** are produced inside the fruiting body. Spores make new fungi, serving the same function as seeds in plants. But they are much smaller and simpler.

SPORES, SPORES, AND MORE SPORES

Spores are tiny, so small that scientists measure them in units called microns. To give you an idea of size, there are 25,000 microns in 1 inch (2.5 centimeters), and most spores are only 5 to 10 microns big! As many as 5,000 spores, each placed on top of the other, would equal 1 inch. Although they are small, spores give many fungi their distinctive coloring. Moldy bread looks black and fuzzy because of the millions of tiny spores that are released.

Most fungi produce enormous numbers of spores. A single field mushroom may produce two billion spores, and some bracket fungi can release twenty million spores a

SPORE CLASSIFICATION CLUES

* *

Because fungal spores come in many different colors, shapes, and sizes, mycologists often use them to help identify and classify different species of fungi. Spores may be black, bright red, pink, purple, brown, blue, or green. Some are egg shaped, some are shaped like bananas. Some have thick walls, some thin. Some are covered with bumps, others smooth. Fungi that live in the water may produce spores with flagella. These are like tails that move back and forth, allowing the spores to swim.

Rhizopus

Alternaria conida

Penicillium

A variety of spores . . .

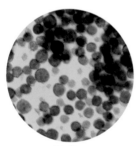

Fuligo

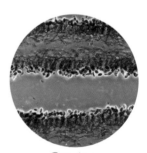

Coprinus

Aspergillus

minute! Most spores never germinate. If they all did, the earth would be covered with fungi.

Many fungi can produce spores with only one parent. This is **asexual reproduction**. The new organisms that develop from these spores are exactly like their parent. Other fungi produce spores with two parents. This is **sexual reproduction**. The fungi that develop from these spores have traits from both parents, but are not exactly like either one. Many fungi can produce spores in both ways.

To reproduce successfully, a fungus must scatter its spores. If spores all fell close to their parent, they would compete with one another for food and living space, and few would survive. Many fungi can drop or shoot spores into the air. Part of the fruiting body swells and then explodes, and the spores are shot off in a stream of liquid. Spores are spread in many of the same ways that plants spread their seeds—they are scattered by birds, insects, rain, and wind. Animals and even people also spread them around.

Colorful puffballs release a cloud of spores when struck by raindrops.

Spores can survive extreme conditions such as severe cold and drying out, which would prevent normal fungal cells from growing. When conditions are just right, the spores begin to grow into fungi. Some fungal spores have germinated successfully after twenty years of dormancy.

After spores are released, the fruiting bodies often die and begin to decay. But the mycelium lives on to produce more fruiting bodies.

ARE YOU ALLERGIC?

✳✳

Do you sneeze and have a runny nose at certain times of the year? Many people with "hay fever" are sensitive to pollens released by plants in the spring or summer. But some of them, and people who sniffle and sneeze in the fall or winter, may be allergic to mold spores.

CLASSIFYING FUNGI

Scientists divide fungi into groups according to their basic structure and the way they reproduce. In some fungi, scientists have never observed sexual reproduction. These fungi, including ringworm fungi, wilt fungi, and gray molds, are lumped together in a category called fungi imperfecti. Other fungi are grouped in one of a number of categories, depending on the way their spores are produced. There is some disagreement among scientists as to how many different groups fungi should be divided into, and even whether certain types should be considered fungi or protists.

In this book we'll go along with one of the modern classification schemes, which classifies fungi into three subkingdoms: **Gymnomycota** (slime molds), **Dimastigomycota** (water molds), and **Eumycota** (most of the fungus species, including mushrooms and yeast). These subkingdoms include the following phyla:

Myxomycota (acellular slime molds): a slimy, creeping mass; spores produce a single cell with flagella

Acrasiomycota (cellular slime molds): similar to Myxomycota but with separate cells

Oomycota (egglike fungi): single cells or a mass of threadlike hyphae; includes water molds, downy mildew, and potato blight

Chytridiomycota (little pot fungi): single cells or branching hyphae with rhizoids; includes parasites on algae, fungi, plant pollens, and insect larvae

Zygomycota (yoke fungi): branched mycelium produces spores in rounded spore cases; includes bread mold, dung fungi, and predatory fungi

Ascomycota (sac fungi): single cells or mycelium; spores form in sacs called asci; includes yeasts, blue and green molds, powdery mildews, and cup fungi (truffles, morels)

Basidiomycota (club fungi): mycelium produces spores on the outside of club-shaped structures called basidia; includes bracket fungi, mushrooms and toadstools, puffballs, stinkhorns, rusts, and smuts

Deuteromycota (imperfect fungi): fungi for which no sexual reproduction is known; includes ringworm, leaf spot, fruit rot, and *Aspergillus*

Mycophycota (lichens): mutually beneficial associations of fungi and algae

4
****

PRIME SLIME

****

Slime molds are jellylike masses that "creep" or slowly flow over rotten wood. In the acellular slime molds (phylum Myxomycota), the slimy shape that we see contains many nuclei, but the slime-mold cells are not separated by cell walls. During this creeping stage, slime molds are very different from other types of fungi in several ways. They have characteristics more like traditional animals than plants. They resemble microscopic protists, such as amebas, that are able to move on their own. The slime-mold cells feed on bacteria and bits of organic matter, such as animal remains and decaying leaves, by engulfing them. The slimy jelly flows around the food until it is completely surrounded, then produces chemicals called enzymes to digest it into simple substances. (All other fungi digest foods outside of their bodies.) For this reason, many scientists place the 450 kinds of slime molds in the kingdom **Protista**, not with fungi.

Slime molds may be white, yellow, or gray and are usually branched or veined. You can see them in spring and early summer, when it is wet and warm. You'll find them under decaying logs or fallen trees. You can see how fast the mold grows by placing a nail or a pin at the edge of the slime mold and checking it daily to see how far it has crept past the pin.

When conditions are just right, the slime mold will change from this creeping stage to a spore-forming stage. The individ-

Yellow slime mold (Physarum polycephalum) *growing on decaying wood*

Chocolate tube slime mold Stemonite splendens (above) *produces spores* (left) *that do not resemble the adult fungus.*

ual slime cells join to form large spore-bearing structures. You can watch this happen. Break off a piece of rotting wood that has slime mold growing on it and put it into an open jar. The wood will begin to dry out, and when it does you will notice that the mold seems to be growing in lumps. The lumps will grow into interesting shapes and will become darker. Tiny **sporangia** (spore cases) develop over the surface. The sporangia have many different shapes, too. Some are knobbed, some look like tiny plumes. Some even look like birdcages on stands. When the spore case matures, it bursts open, releasing spores into the air.

Cellular slime molds belong to the phylum Acrasiomycota. During the first stage of life, cellular slime molds are made up of individual ameba-like cells that engulf bacteria and other food particles. As long as conditions are right, the cellular slime mold can remain in this stage, but when conditions change, the individual slime-mold cells group together and form fruiting structures that produce spores. In this stage the cellular slime mold looks similar to the acellular slime mold, but unlike the myxomycote, each individual cellular slime-mold cell has its own membrane around the cell. Acellular and cellular slime molds have often been placed in the same phylum because they look so similar, but biologists have found they are so different that some classify them in separate kingdoms!

5
****
ANOTHER MISPLACED PHYLUM?
****

The water molds and their land-living relatives in phylum Oomycota may look like fungi, but many scientists think they really are more like plants or protists. They don't have chlorophyll and cannot make their own food, but they have cell walls made of cellulose, just as plants do. Their chromosomes (the microscopic structures containing the genetic instructions for the species) are also more like those of plants and quite different from the typical fungal chromosomes.

When members of this phylum reproduce asexually, they form tiny spores that swim by lashing a flagellum back and forth like a whip. They can also reproduce sexually, and the way they do this is what gives the phylum its name. *Oomycota* means "egg fungi," but these molds don't look like eggs. Instead, the name refers to the fact that they have two very different kinds of sex cells: the **egg**, which is a rather large cell, and the **sperm**, which is smaller and can swim using two flagella. The egg and sperm join to form a thick-walled **oospore** ("egg spore"), which can produce a new organism when conditions are right.

In some oomycotes the same individual produces both eggs and sperm. Others have separate sexes—some individual molds produce male sex cells (sperm) and others are females and produce eggs. These molds can't reproduce unless male and female hyphae get together.

WATER MOLDS

Practically any pond, stream, or other accumulation of freshwater (even a puddle!) probably contains some water molds. Most of them are saprophytes that feed on bits of dead or decaying matter. But some are parasites that grow on the bodies of fish and their eggs. (If you ever had a goldfish that got sick and developed yucky-looking spots on its body, it probably had water molds.)

MILDEWS AND BLIGHTS

Water molds spend their whole lives in the water, but some of their relatives have adapted to life on the land. (The land-dwelling oomycotes can still form swimming spores when water is available.) Some of them live as parasites on plants and produce plant diseases called downy mildews and blights.

A LUCKY OBSERVATION

In the late 1870s, downy mildew almost wiped out the entire French wine industry. Then a professor from the University of Bordeaux noticed that the grapevines around Médoc were still healthy. By talking to the vineyard owners, he discovered that they treated the vines growing near the roadsides with an unpleasant-tasting mixture of copper sulfate and lime to keep people passing by from stealing the grapes. The professor tried the mixture on sick grapevines, and it cured them! (The chemicals killed the mold.) This "Bordeaux mixture" was the first chemical ever used to control a plant disease.

These molds can cause enormous amounts of damage. One genus of blight molds is named *Phytophthora*, which means "plant destroyer." There are about thirty-five species in this genus, and they really live up to their name, infesting plants producing pineapples, tomatoes, rubber, onions, strawberries, apples, soybeans, tobacco, and citrus fruits, among others. One very widespread species has killed millions of avocado trees in

A blight mold has killed millions of avocado trees such as this one.

THE MOLD THAT CHANGED HISTORY

* *

The potato-blight fungus, *Phytophthora infestans*, hit hard in Ireland in 1845 and gradually spread through the country; in a single week in the summer of 1846, the blight wiped out the entire Irish potato crop. More than one million people died of starvation during the great potato famine. (As told in a popular song by Sinead O'Connor, potatoes were the only food the Irish farmers were allowed to eat; the lands were owned by people in England, who exported all the other plant crops, as well as meat and dairy products.) Several million Irish people emigrated to the United States—including the great-grandparents of John F. Kennedy, who became our thirty-fifth president.

Phytophthora infestans is the fungus that caused the destruction of the Irish potato crop in 1845 and 1846. It caused leaf decay (above) and rotten potatoes (right).

southern California and destroyed valuable eucalyptus forests in Australia. This mold lives in the soil. Its asexual spores are attracted by chemicals produced by plant roots and swim to them through the soil moisture. The sexually produced spores can survive for up to six years in the soil, waiting for just the right plant.

LIFE AMONG THE CHYTRIDS

Another group of water molds, phylum Chytridiomycota, presents a real puzzle for taxonomists. Like fungi, chytrids have cell walls containing chitin. But their reproductive cells swim using a single whiplike **flagellum**—just like the flagellates, a group of animal-like protists. Some chytrids remain single-celled all their lives and never form a mycelium. Others of these protistlike chytrids do form threadlike rhizoids, which act like roots to anchor them. Most chytrids are parasites, feeding on algae, water molds, pollen grains, or insect larvae. Members of one genus, *Coelomyces*, feed on the larvae of mosquitoes and flies. Scientists hope to use these chytrids to control the insect pests.

Other chytrids have a much more complex life cycle. *Allomyces macrogynus*, for example, alternates between separate generations. Reproductive cells called **zoospores** sprout into hyphae that form two kinds of reproductive structures called **gametangia** (swellings in which sex cells, or **gametes**, form). When the sex cells are released into the water, colorless female gametes secrete a hormone that attracts the smaller, orange male gametes. Pairs of male and female gametes join to form zygotes, which lose their flagella and sprout into a new mycelium. These hyphae form two kinds of spore cases. Colorless asexual sporangia produce zoospores that sprout into hyphae just like their parent. Reddish-brown sexual sporangia are thick walled and very hardy. They can survive even if the pond or puddle dries up or freezes over. Later their zoospores start the life cycle over again, sprouting into the type of mycelium that forms male and female gametes.

6
****

BLACK MOLDS

****

Most of the six hundred kinds of zygomycotes live in soil and feed on dead plant and animal matter. Some are parasites of plants, insects, or small animals. These fungi are grouped into this phylum because they produce thick-walled spores, called **zygospores**, that develop from a **zygote** (a special cell that is produced when two sex cells join together). The name of the phylum comes from the Greek word *zygon*, which means "yoke" or "joining."

Zygofungi can reproduce sexually or asexually. In sexual reproduction, the ends of special tubes "kiss." Then the tubes grow together and form a zygospore. Spores can also be produced asexually. Spores grow off the top and are carried away in the breeze.

OPPOSITES ATTRACT
****

It's hard to think of the two threadlike filaments called hyphae that join in sexual reproduction of zygomycotes as "male" and "female" because they look exactly the same. So scientists call them "+" and "−." Hormones make the hyphae come together.

ARE THERE BLACK-MOLD SPORES HIDING IN YOUR HOME?

Black bread mold (*Rhizopus stolonifer*) is the best known of the zygomycotes. It is commonly found growing on bread and fruit. To find out whether there are black-mold spores in your house, rub a slice of fresh bread or a cut piece of fruit on a dusty surface, or just expose it to the air for an hour, then place it in a warm, dark place inside a closed jar or plastic bag. (If you use bread from a store, make sure the label says "No preservatives added." Most packaged baked goods have chemicals added to stop mold growth.) When you check it after a few days, you should see mold that looks like white cotton.

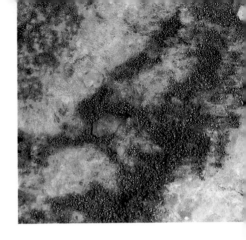

Soon it will be black as the spores ripen. Try wiping bits of the mold on different kinds of food and placing them in different environments (in the dark, under a lamp, or on a sunny windowsill; in warm and cool places; in a closed jar, or exposed to the air, allowing the sample to dry out). From these experiments you can find out which kinds of food the mold can use and what growing conditions are good or bad for it.

Bread mold (Rhizopus stolonifer)

When you look at bread mold with a magnifying glass, you can see many small lollipop-shaped structures sticking up from the mycelium. These are the sporangia. When they are mature they burst open, and tiny spores, each the size of a speck of dust, float up into the air. When spores land on another piece of food, a new mass of mycelium develops. The spores are so tiny that they can remain in the air for a long time and be carried long distances on air currents—sometimes thousands of miles, even across oceans.

READY . . . AIM . . . FIRE!

The "hat thrower" fungus, which grows in animal dung, has a surefire way to make certain its spores wind up somewhere where they will be eaten by an animal. A part of the fungus's reproductive organ acts like a lens to focus the sun's rays on another part of its body that is sensitive to light. This causes the reproductive organ to grow toward the light. Meanwhile, the reproductive structure absorbs water. The water causes the pressure to build up until the spore case bursts open, shooting spores out at a speed of 31 miles (50 kilometers) an hour. They travel about 6.5 feet (2 meters) away from the parent fungus. This doesn't seem like very much, but the tiny spores are only 80 micrometers big. More than 150 spores could fit on the head of a pin. Because the reproductive organ grows toward the light, the chances are very good that the spores will land on grass or other vegetation, which may be eaten by an animal. The spores' tough covering protects them as they pass through the animal's digestive tract and out in its feces. There the dung fungus starts its life cycle all over again.

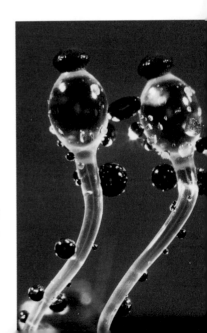

The tiny black caps on this greatly magnified hat thrower fungus (Pilogolus crystallinus) *are spore cases almost ready to burst.*

7

****

SAC FUNGI

****

There are about 25,000 different kinds of sac fungi. In addition there are another 25,000 species that are found only in lichens. This phylum, Ascomycota, is by far the largest division of kingdom Fungi, and it is also one of the most varied. Its members range from microscopic single cells to fungi 12 inches (about 30 centimeters) tall. The sexual spores of sac fungi develop inside tiny saclike structures called **asci** (**ascus** is the singular). The asexual spores of Ascomycota are very tiny and are called **conidia**, which comes from the Greek word for dust.

The elm bark beetle spreads the fungus that causes Dutch elm disease.

Many sac fungi are parasites of plants. They cause powdery mildew diseases in many plants, including chestnut blight, Dutch elm disease, and ergot diseases of cereal grasses. But this group also includes some valuable types, such as yeasts and edible mushroomlike forms. A number of common bread molds are sac fungi, too. Experiments with the red bread mold, *Neurospora crassa*, led to some important discoveries in modern genetics.

Dutch elm disease is caused by a European sac fungus, *Ceratocystis ulmi*. It is spread by elm bark beetles, which carry the fungus on their bodies as they fly from infected trees to healthy ones. The fungus grows through the tree's protective bark and blocks the tubes inside the trunk that carry water throughout the tree. This eventually kills the tree. Millions of elm trees have been killed by this fungus in North America and Europe.

A FUNGUS THAT MAKES PEOPLE CRAZY

When rye or barley plants are infected by the ergot fungus, banana-shaped bodies grow in place of flowers, destroying the developing seeds or grains. The fungus rarely causes serious damage to the crop itself. But it can be dangerous to animals or people who eat even a small amount of it. Symptoms of **ergotism** are very serious, including convulsions, psychotic delusions, nerve spasms, and gangrene. During the Middle Ages, ergot poisoning was a major problem and was called Saint Anthony's fire. Drugs made from ergot make muscles and blood vessels contract and are used to treat migraine headaches. The illegal drug LSD is made from the ergot fungus.

USEFUL YEASTS

Most single-celled creatures belong to the protist kingdom, but yeasts are an important exception. These small oval, or egg-shaped, cells are about 0.0002 inch (5 micrometers) long and are classified as sac fungi. When conditions are right, yeasts can produce spores, but they nearly always reproduce by **budding**. A bulge forms on a yeast cell, and the cell wall grows between the bud and the rest of the cell, separating them. Then the bud grows into a new, full-sized yeast cell. The two cells may separate, but sometimes they stay together, eventually forming chains like necklaces of beads. Yeasts are

DID YOU KNOW?
****
When scientists raise fruit flies in the laboratory, they grow the larvae on mashed bananas. The fly larvae don't eat bananas—they eat the yeasts that feed on the rotting bananas.

The fruit fly Drosophila melanogaster *reproduces rapidly and is very useful in heredity studies. The fly larvae feed on yeasts.*

adapted to living in places with a high sugar content, such as in the nectar of flowers or on the surface of fruits.

How does yeast make bread rise? When yeasts digest sugar in the bread dough, they produce alcohol and the gas carbon dioxide. When the dough is baked, trapped bubbles of carbon dioxide expand, making the bread fluffy. Alcohol evaporates during baking. (You won't get drunk by eating bread!) When special strains of yeasts are grown on grains, fruits, or vegetables, the alcohol they form remains in the liquid product. That is how alcoholic beverages such as beer and wine are made.

Yeast is often used as a food supplement for both people and farm animals, providing a rich source of protein and B vitamins. Someday yeast may be a major food source, grown in huge vats and processed to give it attractive textures and tastes.

GOURMET DELIGHTS—MORELS AND TRUFFLES

Many mushroomlike fungi are also placed in the sac fungi group. The cup fungi that can be found growing on dead trees or on soil are one example. Cup fungi have cup-shaped fruiting bodies. Some cup fungi, such as the morel mushroom, are edible.

Unlike most fungi, truffles form round, lumpy fruiting bodies that grow underground. The fruiting body gives off a strong odor when the spores are ripe. Animals like mice and squirrels smell the truffles and dig them up to eat them. The spores are not

Hunting for truffles in France

digested by their bodies but pass out with their droppings. In this way they are spread far away from the parent fungi. In Europe and the United States, truffles are considered delicacies. In France, a major exporter of truffles, they are found by specially trained pigs or dogs.

8

****

JOIN THE CLUB

****

Club fungi got their name because their spores are produced inside club-shaped reproductive structures called **basidia**. The 20,000 species of club fungi can be divided into two smaller groups. One is made up of parasites such as rusts and **smuts**. The other group contains mushrooms—the best-known fungi—as well as puffballs and bracket fungi. The phylum they belong to is Basidiomycota. This chapter deals with club fungi parasites.

RUSTS AND SMUTS

Rusts and smuts cause many serious cereal-grain diseases. Many of these fungi produce several types of spores during various stages in their life cycles. Scientists identify different species by examining their spores and the types of plants they infect.

Smuts were named for the tremendous number of black spores that are produced in a sooty mass. These fungi attack the flowers of grasses and cereals such as corn and wheat.

More than three hundred species of rusts infect wheat plants, beets, cherries, corn, oats, pears, peas, and rye, as well as coffee trees, fig trees, hemlocks, and pines. Rusts damage the leaves so that the plant loses water and can't make food; eventually the plant dies.

Rusts often have very complicated life cycles, with as many as five stages in which different kinds of spores are produced, germinating only if they land on a specific kind of plant. Wheat-rust spores, for example, are produced on infected wheat plants in late spring. These rust-colored spores are carried to neighboring wheat plants and grow into new wheat-rust fungi, which produce another batch of rust-colored spores that infect

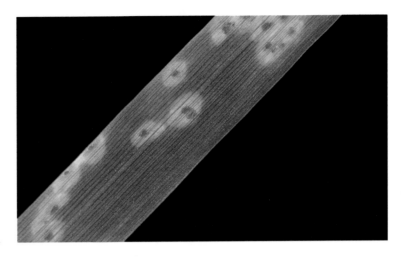

Wheat leaf rust Puccinia recondita

more plants. In the early fall, the fungus produces black spores, which have a thick covering to survive through the winter. When spring arrives, each black spore produces four new spores, which are carried in the air. If they land on the leaves of the barberry plant, a common wild shrub, they begin to produce hyphae. Then a third type of spore is produced. This can infect wheat plants, starting the cycle all over again. To fight this fungus, farmers try to eliminate wild barberry. Scientists have also developed strains of wheat that are able to resist infection from fungi.

TOXIC AVENGER
* *

White-rot fungus produces a powerful enzyme that can break down the tough fibers in wood. This enzyme is so strong that scientists are exploring the possibility of using this fungus to get rid of toxic wastes such as dioxin, DDT, and many organic pollutants.

FAKE FLOWER FUNGI

In Colorado a rust fungus called *Puccinia* infects rock-cress plants. The fungus causes the rock-cress plant to grow taller than normal and produce a cluster of leaves on top. The bright yellow fungus covers the leaves, making them look like buttercup flowers. The fungus also secretes a sugary solution that smells like the nectar produced by a real flower. When insects come to drink the nectar, fungal sex cells stick to their bodies. Then the insects travel to other fake flowers, and the fungal sex cells drop off. Spores are produced when two sex cells join. When the spores are ripe, they are released into the air. If they land on a rock-cress plant, they can start the life cycle all over again.

9
****
FAMILIAR CLUB MEMBERS
****

Mushrooms are the most familiar of all fungi. They have always been part of legends and folklore because in some ways they seem magical. They can spring up overnight when the conditions are just right, then shrivel up and disappear almost as quickly.

Mushrooms are found in woods and fields in warm, moist weather. They may be white, brown, red, orange, or pastel colors. They come in many sizes and shapes. The most common is a thick, short stem with an umbrella-like cap on top. The "umbrella" provides protection from the rain and the heat of the sun. The stem places the spore-producing part of the mushroom above the ground so that the spores will have a better chance of being carried off in the wind.

*Mushrooms form a variety of caps. Above: Scarlet waxy cap (*Hygrophorus coccineus*). Right: Shaggymane (*Coprinus comatus*). Far right: Boletus longicurvipes*

A gill mushroom is a typical mushroom. The main part lies underground. When there is warmth and moisture, swellings appear on the mycelium. These grow quickly and push through the soil, each forming a mushroom with a stalk and cap. On the underside of the cap are thin partitions called **gills**. Tremendous numbers of spores are formed in these gills. An average mushroom can produce two billion spores! They pop out of the gills. Although they move only a tiny fraction of a millimeter, it is enough so that they will be dispersed by the breeze.

The spore-forming gills on the underside of the caps of these fuzzy foot mushrooms are clearly visible.

SUPER MUSHROOMS

✳✳

When mushrooms push up out of the ground, they produce an incredible amount of pressure. Mushrooms have been known to break through three-inch-thick asphalt floors and to raise concrete slabs several inches into the air!

ENCHANTED MUSHROOMS

Sometimes you can find mushrooms growing in a circle in a grassy area. These are called fairy rings. Many people used to believe that fairies danced in circles and wore down the grass so that mushrooms could grow.

About once a year, when the weather conditions are just right, the fruiting bodies of a fairy-ring mushroom pop up in a circle. The mushrooms shrivel and die after producing new spores, but the mycelium underground continues to grow outward. New

Boletus sp. *mushrooms grow in a circle that is commonly called a fairy ring.*

mushrooms pop up at the edges of the mycelium. Each year the fairy ring grows wider and wider. Taking into account how much a mycelium grows each year, scientists have determined that some fairy rings have been growing for hundreds of years. The rings of some fairy-ring mushrooms in Kansas are more than 600 feet (183 meters) wide—each ring of mushrooms came from a spore that germinated around the time Christopher Columbus arrived in the Americas!

POISONOUS OR DELICIOUS?

Many gill mushrooms are edible and people eat them, usually combined with vegetable and meat dishes or in salads. However, be warned—*certain mushrooms are poisonous.*

Some people think that only brightly colored mushrooms are dangerous. But a number of the seventy kinds of poisonous mushrooms look very much like edible ones. Often only an expert can tell the difference. **So it is very dangerous to eat wild mushrooms.** People have died from eating only a piece of the cap of a poisonous mushroom.

The six kinds of deadly **amanitas** are the most poisonous. The destroying angel is snowy white. The fly agaric has a red-orange cap with white bumps. (It was once used as a fly killer; pieces were left out in dishes of milk for flies to lap up.) Death cap has a yellowish-green streaky cap. Other poisonous mushrooms also have descriptive names, including sweating mushroom, big laughing mushroom, and panther amanita.

The *Psilocybe* mushrooms that grow in Mexico cause hallucinations when they are eaten. (They are used to produce visions in some Native American religious ceremonies.) Other mushrooms that look like them can be deadly.

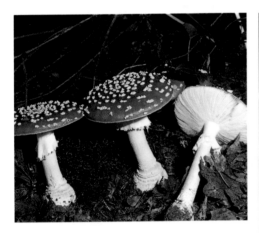

These are among the most poisonous mushrooms. Above: Fly agaric. Right: Death cap. Far right: Panther amanita.

YUMMY MUSHROOMS

Store-bought mushrooms are grown in controlled conditions from pieces of mushroom mycelia. The most popular types are common or field mushrooms, oyster mushrooms, shiitake mushrooms, and straw mushrooms. (Shiitake mushrooms have long been grown in Asia, but now they are popular all over the world. Recent studies suggest that they may contain some cancer-fighting chemicals.) Some kinds of mushrooms are rare and are prized by chefs. The chanterelle mushroom, for example, has a yellow, funnel-shaped cap and smells like an apricot.

The shaggymane ink cap has a long, thin cap that is covered with shaggy scales. Some people eat it as a substitute for asparagus. (Only the young, all-white caps are edible.) This was one of the mushrooms eaten by ancient Romans, and it is found all around the world. Ink caps have an unusual way of dispersing spores—the cap dissolves into an inky liquid.

EAT ME PLEASE, I'M A MUSHROOM

Not only people, but also cows, deer, mice, pigs, rabbits, squirrels, insects, snails, and slugs eat mushrooms. Even meat eaters like bears and wolves sometimes eat them. These fungi eaters don't kill the fungus because they eat only the fruiting body. In fact, mushrooms are designed to be eaten so that animals can spread their spores around. When the fruiting body is bitten off, the mycelium, safe underground, continues to produce new fruiting bodies.

TO BE OR NOT TO BE A MUSHROOM . . .

Some people call all edible fungi mushrooms, and poisonous ones **toadstools**. But scientists do not divide fungi in this way, and they do not use the term *toadstool* at all. Technically, only gill fungi are mushrooms. Other fungi such as puffballs can be eaten, but they are not mushrooms.

Pore fungi are closely related to gill fungi. Often they look like mushrooms, but their spores are released from tiny pores, not from gills. Pore fungi include the many different types of bracket fungi (also called shelf fungi) that grow on trees or wooden buildings and often cause serious damage.

Bracket fungi look like shelves. Some grow up to 1.5 feet (about 0.5 meter) wide. The tops are sometimes smooth or tough like wood. The undersides contain the pores that produce and release spores. Some kinds of bracket fungi attack only a particular kind of tree. They also come in many colors, such as brown or orange. The beefsteak bracket looks like a piece of uncooked steak!

Oyster mushrooms are large shelf fungi that are sometimes called "the shellfish of the woods." Some mushroom lovers consider them the tastiest wild fungi. Another shelf fungus is called chicken-of-the-woods because its flesh looks like cooked chicken. Not all shelf fungi are good to eat, though; unless you're a mushroom expert, it's best to stick to the ones sold in food stores.

Sulfur shelf fungus (Laetiporus sulphureus) *is a colorful bracket fungus.*

Unlike most other fruiting bodies, brackets last for months or even years. Most bracket fungi spread their spores only when the weather is damp, but the common ganoderm spreads spores day and night for up to half of the year.

Puffball mushrooms are pore fungi that are round like globes and range from an inch wide to the size of a basketball. Giant puffballs may be nearly 3 feet (1 meter) wide! Inside is a white tissue that can be eaten. When the inside turns brown, spores are produced and the fungus is no longer edible. This fungus got its name because

A giant puffball (Calvatia sp.)

when it is ripe the top breaks open, and the slightest breeze or raindrop causes clouds of tiny spores to puff out like smoke.

The bird's-nest fungus, found growing on dead wood, looks like a tiny bird's nest with eggs. (Each fruiting body is only the size of a pea!) Raindrops splashing into the "nests" spread the spores of this puffball.

Raindrops also help to disperse spores of earthstars, which look like stars that have fallen onto the soil of the forest floor. An earthstar's fruiting body begins to crack when there is enough moisture. It splits into rays like the arms of a starfish. In the center is a spore sac. When a drop of water touches the thin walls of the spore sac, the pressure causes spores to shoot out the top of the sac. When the weather is too dry, the outer rays close back over the spore sac to protect it until the next rain.

Stinkhorns are also grouped with mushrooms and bracket fungi. They do not have caps. The tops of the stalks are swollen and covered with globs of slime that contains thousands of spores. The slime smells like a dead animal. This is very unpleasant to humans but smells delicious to beetles and flies. When the insects step into the slime, spores stick to their bodies and are dropped off somewhere else. Some stinkhorns are brightly colored, with flower-shaped tops to attract insects.

MUSHROOM WARNINGS

For many years naturalists have kept records of the numbers and sizes of many kinds of mushrooms in European forests. Today, there are fewer of many kinds of mushrooms in these forests than there were in the past. The mushrooms that are left are also smaller than they were. Is pollution to blame? Scientists think that this change may now harm the forest ecosystems because many trees depend on mushrooms to keep them healthy. It is not certain whether the same thing is happening in North America because no one has kept records of wild-mushroom sizes and populations for as long as they have been kept in Europe.

HUNTING FOR FUNGI

In the northern United States, fall is the best time to look for fungi. Note where they are growing, whether in the grass or on a specific type of tree, or on the ground or on dead tree stumps. Make drawings or take photos to help you identify them from a book. Note the shapes, colors, and textures, but *don't taste them*—they could be poisonous.

Remember, many edible mushrooms look very similar to poisonous species; only experts can tell them apart.

MUSHROOM ART

* *

You can make spore prints from mushrooms. Cut the stalk away from the mushroom close to the cap. Place the cap, gill side down, on a piece of white or black paper. (You'll have to experiment to choose paper that will show the spores best.) Place a jar or bowl over the mushroom cap and leave it for several hours. Then carefully remove the bowl and the cap, and you will see the pattern made by the falling spores. The pattern will be just like the pattern of the gill slits under the mushroom cap. Spore prints are not only pretty—they can also help to identify mushrooms.

10

****

ORPHAN FUNGI

****

The 25,000 species of fungi that are placed in the phylum Deuteromycota do not really have much in common. They share some features, but their ancestors were probably not all that closely related. They are just a group of miscellaneous fungi grouped together because they don't really belong anywhere else. The one thing that these "imperfect" fungi share is that they either don't have a form of sexual reproduction, or scientists have yet to see them reproduce sexually.

CHEESE MOLDS THAT SAVE LIVES

The next time you notice a patch of blue or green mold on a piece of cheese, think of the Scottish scientist Alexander Fleming. One day in 1928 he noticed that some culture dishes in which he was growing bacteria were covered with green spots. Spores of a sac fungus called *Penicillium notatum* had fallen on the dishes and sprouted into molds. Instead of throwing away the spoiled dishes, Fleming took a closer look. Wherever the mold was, there were no bacteria. A chemical produced by the fungus had killed them. Fleming isolated the chemical and named it penicillin; it was the first antibiotic. Since then, penicillin and other fungus products have saved millions of people from bacterial diseases.

DID YOU KNOW?

****

People who are allergic to penicillin will probably be allergic to Camembert and Roquefort cheeses, too, because these cheeses get their flavor from *Penicillium* molds.

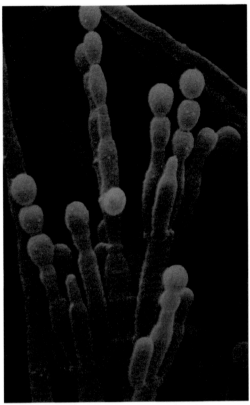

All kinds of penicillin are obtained from molds of Penicillium, *which grows from spores such as those shown here.*

Spores of Aspergillus, *a mold that produces citric acid, which is used to give a lemony flavor to a number of products*

OTHER FUNGI FRIENDS AND FOES

Cyclosporine is made by an imperfect fungus that lives in the soil. This chemical has also been useful in medicine. When people receive organ transplants, their bodies may reject the "foreign" organs. Cyclosporine has been used to keep the body from building up defenses against transplanted hearts and other organs. The drug has helped to greatly increase the success of heart transplants.

Aspergillus, a type of brown mold, doesn't help save human lives, but it is often used to produce the citric acid that gives candies and soft drinks a lemony flavor, as well as to make soy sauce and a Japanese alcoholic drink called sake.

Not all imperfect fungi are useful to humans. Ringworm infects humans and causes rashes. When it infects the feet, it is called athlete's foot. Barber's itch affects the skin around the face. Jock itch affects the groin area. The fungi that cause these skin problems are able to digest the protein keratin, which is found in skin, hair, and nails.

FEROCIOUS FUNGI COWBOYS AND TRAPPERS

A number of imperfect fungi are fierce predators. They trap tiny roundworms, insects, or microscopic protists that live in the soil. Some have cells that form rings (like the

*A lollipop fungus (*Arthrobytris dactyloides*) has trapped a worm and will eventually digest it.*

noose of a lasso) attached to their hyphae. When a roundworm crawls through one of these rings, the cells swell and grip the roundworm so tightly that it can't wriggle free. One of these fungi is called the nefarious noose fungus. Another preying fungus is called the lethal lollipop fungus. This fungus has sticky knobs attached to its hyphae. A victim passing by becomes glued in place. Then other hyphae grow into the victim's body and digest it.

11

* * * * * * * *

PARTNERSHIPS

* * * * * * * *

Lichens are unusual creatures. These members of phylum Mycophycota resemble simple plants such as moss, but they are not a single organism. Instead, they are really a meshwork of two different kinds of living things. A lichen is made up of a fungus and a green alga that live together. (Some fungi form lichens with cyanobacteria—a kind of bacteria that make their own food.) The alga in a lichen contains chlorophyll and makes food using sunlight energy. It makes enough food for itself and for the fungus. The fungus makes acids that roughen the surface the lichen grows on. Without the acids, a lichen would not be able to anchor itself firmly to a hard, stony surface. The fungus also holds moisture, allowing its alga partner to survive in dry places.

Lichens are found in many climates around the world, even in places where plants and other living things cannot survive. They can be seen in dry, hot deserts; in the freezing Arctic; and high up on windswept mountains. They can grow on soil, bare rocks, trees, and even fence posts.

Multicolored lichens almost obscure these Arctic rocks.

LICHEN COLONISTS

Our world is constantly changing. Places that were once barren and lifeless have become habitats filled with many life-forms. Lichens are often the first colonists in bare, rocky areas. Slowly, over long periods of time, the barren, rocky surfaces are changed into soil, in which plants such as mosses and ferns can grow. Then more changes occur, and more life can thrive.

Lichens grow very slowly, often less than 0.4 inch (1 centimeter) each year. Some lichen growths are very thick, and scientists believe they may be thousands of years old!

LICHEN WHO'S WHO

Many of the green algae and cyanobacteria that are found in lichens are also commonly found living by themselves, without fungi. Scientists believe that the fungi found in lichens also have a free-living stage, but the free-living fungi usually cannot be identified until after they have formed lichens.

In nearly all of the 25,000 species of lichens, the fungal partner is a sac fungus (an ascomycote). About a dozen species of club fungi can also form lichen partnerships. Two genera of green algae and one cyanobacterium are the most common food-producing partners; one of these three is found in 90 percent of all lichens. The other 10 percent of lichens have representatives from twenty-three living genera.

There are three main types of lichens, grouped according to the way they look when they grow. **Crustose lichens** are flat and crusty. **Foliose lichens** look like small leaves crowded together. **Fruticose lichens** form bunches of twisting branches or look like tiny shrubs.

FREEZER FOOD
****

There are more than 350 species of lichens and only two species of plants in the Antarctic. Reindeer moss grows in extremely cold areas of the world; in Arctic regions it is the main source of food for animals such as caribou and reindeer. This "moss" is really a lichen.

MAKING NEW LICHENS

Lichens most often reproduce by accident: pieces containing both fungal and algal cells break off and grow into a whole new lichen. Sometimes a new lichen can be formed when a lichen fungus captures an alga or cyanobacterium. The fungus actually pene-

Crustose lichen

Foliose lichen

Fruticose lichen

trates the cell wall of the alga. Sometimes this kills the captured alga or cyanobacterium; then the fungus dies, too. But if the captured organism lives, a lichen is formed.

LISTEN TO THE LICHEN

Lichens do not need a source of organic food as fungi do because they get food from the alga partner. Unlike algae, lichens can stay alive even when they become dried up. All they need is air, light, and a few minerals. They obtain some minerals from the surface

****

For years scientists had thought the lichen was a perfect example of a completely symbiotic relationship. Now many have changed their minds. When lichens are experimentally separated in the laboratory, the alga partner grows more quickly on its own, and the fungus grows more slowly. These findings have led biologists to conclude that the fungus is really a parasite. But when lichens live in an environment where neither the alga nor the fungus could survive on its own, clearly the relationship is best for both partners. In fact, the scientists could get them to rejoin only when the conditions would not support either one separately.

to which they attach, but most come from the air and the rain. Lichens absorb materials very quickly from falling rain. If there is a lot of pollution in an area, they will also absorb these toxic materials, which can kill them. For this reason scientists find that lichens are a good indicator of how polluted a particular environment is. If the lichens in an area die, scientists know the air is very polluted there.

When the lichens that grew on trees in England died because of pollution during the industrial revolution of the 1800s, it affected the entire ecosystem of living things. In fact, it changed the evolution of the peppered moth, which became darker to match the blackened tree trunks.

PLANT PARTNERS

Although many fungi cause plant diseases, others form working partnerships with plants, called mycorrhizae (meaning "fungus roots"). These include various yoke fungi (zygomycotes), club fungi (basidiomycotes), and sac fungi (ascomycotes).

Scientists first realized how important this symbiotic relationship was when they noticed that orchids would not grow unless they were infected with a specific kind of fungus. Later, botanists found that when laboratory-grown forest trees were planted in grassy soils, they would not grow properly. Many died from malnutrition, even though the soil contained enough of the nutrients they needed. Then a tiny amount of forest soil was added to the soil around the roots of the seedlings, and the trees grew normally. Scientists believe that mycorrhizae actually occur in more than 90 percent of plant families.

In order to grow, orchids such as the epiphytic orchid (above) form a partnership with a fungus (left). The fungus is shown as it appears in the orchid roots.

The plant roots give out substances the fungi need, such as sugars and amino acids. In return, the fungi change soil minerals (especially phosphorus) into forms the root can use, and help to bring them into the root. Fungi may also help the roots to take in water.

When scientists studied the fossils of early plants, they found evidence that mycorrhizae occurred as often in prehistoric times as they do now. For this reason it seems that this symbiotic relationship played an important role in allowing plants to grow on the mostly lifeless soils that existed when plants first began to develop on land.

SOME ANTS ARE FUNGUS FARMERS

* *

South American leaf-cutter ants cut up leaves and use them to line special chambers in their underground burrows. A certain kind of fungus grows on the leaves, producing sweet round buttons. The ants pick these fungus products, eat them, and feed them to their larvae. The ants carefully weed out any other types of fungi that would contaminate their crop. When the ants move to a new location, they take some of the fungus spores with them to start a new fungus garden. Other types of ants and beetles also have symbiotic relationships with fungi.

Leaf-cutter ants (Atta cephalotes) grow gardens of Acromyrmex sp. fungus to feed to their larvae.

IDENTIKEY

✳ ✳ ✳ ✳ ✳ ✳ ✳ ✳

Naturalists may use identification keys to help them in identifying various organisms. For example, suppose you found some mushrooms while walking in the woods and wanted to know whether they were good to eat. Here's an "identikey" to help you determine what kind of mushrooms they are and whether it is safe to eat them.

1. White umbrella-shaped cap   **Go to step 2**

    Reddish umbrella-shaped cap   **Go to step 3**

    Yellow umbrella-shaped cap   **Go to step 4**

    Oval cap with honeycomb surface   **Go to step 5**

2. Shining pure white or pinkish cap,   **DO NOT EAT! Probably deadly destroying**
     white stalk, gills, and ring   **angel**

    Velvety white cap, cream to pink gills,   **Probably edible sweetbread mushroom***
    smells like bread dough

3. Smooth or greasy orange-red cap,   **Probably edible American Caesar's**
    yellow stalk, gills, and ring   **mushroom***

    Bright red cap with small white patches,   **DO NOT EAT! Probably deadly fly agaric**
    white stalk, gills, and ring

    Brittle red cap, white gills and stalk,   **Probably emetic russula; bitter, causes vomiting***
    no ring

Red-brown cap with pinkish patches, pinkish-white stalk and ring

Probably edible blusher but may be deadly panther amanita*

Red-brown cap with white patches, white gills, stalk, and ring

DO NOT EAT! Probably deadly panther amanita*

4. Golden yellow cap may be funnel-shaped, ridges on underside, apricot smell

Probably edible chanterelle*

5. Light yellowish-brown oval cap with honeycomb surface, white stalk

Probably edible yellow morel*

---

* Do not eat any wild mushrooms without checking with an expert. The edible ones are easy to confuse with similar-looking poisonous species.

A LITTLE LATIN HELPS

****

Knowing some basic Latin and Greek "building blocks" can help you guess the meaning of scientific terms.

a-	without		*myc(o)-*	fungus
amphi-	both		*myx(o)-*	mucus, slime
asc(o)-	cup		*nona-*	nine
basidi(o)-	club		*oct(a)-*	eight
bi-	two		*-oid*	like
cyano-	blue		*oo-*	egg
deca-	ten		*para-*	beside
di-	two		*penta-*	five
dodeca-	twelve		*-phil*	loving
endo-	inside		*-phor(e)*	carrier
epi-	upon, outer, besides		*phyt(o)-*	plant
eu-	true		*pro-*	before
exo-	outside		*prot(o)-*	first
-fer	carrying		*rhiz(o)-*	root
-form(es)	in the form of, resembling		*sacchar(o)-*	sugar
hepta-	seven		*sapro-*	dead or decaying matter
hetero-	different		*tetra-*	four
hexa-	six		*tri-*	three
homo-	same		*vir-*	poison
mon(o)-	one		*zyg(o)-*	yoke
-morph	*form*			

GLOSSARY

Acrasiomycota — the fungus phylum of cellular slime molds.

amanitas — species of poisonous mushrooms.

antibiotic — a substance produced by microorganisms that kills other microorganisms or stops them from growing.

Ascomycota — sac fungi; a fungus phylum including yeasts, blue and green molds, powdery mildews, and cup fungi (truffles and morels).

ascus (plural **asci**) — a saclike structure in which the sexual spores of a sac fungus develop.

asexual reproduction — a form of reproduction in which one parent produces offspring that are exactly like the parent.

Basidiomycota — club fungi; a fungus phylum including bracket fungi, mushrooms, puffballs, stinkhorns, rusts, and smuts.

basidium (plural **basidia**) — a cup-shaped reproductive structure in which the spores of club fungi form.

binomial nomenclature — the system of scientific naming devised by Carl Linnaeus, in which each organism is assigned a genus and a species name.

bracket fungi — club fungi with a shelflike shape of the fruiting bodies; spores are released from pores.

budding — a form of asexual reproduction that produces a small copy of the parent.

cellulose — a polymer consisting of sugar units that is the main structural material in the cell walls of plants and water molds.

chitin — a polymer containing sugar units, which forms the inner layer of an arthropod's exoskeleton and is the main structural material in fungus cell walls.

chlorophyll — a green pigment used by plants and some algae to trap sunlight energy to convert carbon dioxide and water to sugars and starches.

Chytridiomycota — a fungus phylum of water molds whose reproductive cells each have a single whiplike flagellum.

class — a category in the classification of living organisms (the next smaller after phylum).

classification — the process of dividing objects into related groups.

conidia — the asexual spores of sac fungi.

crustose lichens — lichens with a flat, crusty structure.

decomposition — the breakdown of dead animals and plants into simple compounds.

Deuteromycota — imperfect fungi; a fungus phylum including ringworm, leaf spot, fruit rot, and Aspergillus.

Dimastigomycota — the subkingdom of water molds.

division — in taxonomy, a major category in classification; applied to plants, bacteria, and sometimes to algae and fungi; corresponds to phylum in the animal kingdom.

egg — a female reproductive cell.

ergotism — a disorder caused by poisoning with grain contaminated by the ergot fungus.

Eumycota — the subkingdom of true fungi.

family — a category in the classification of living organisms (the next smaller after order).

flagellum — a whiplike structure that extends from a cell like a tail and lashes back and forth to allow it to move in water.

foliose lichens — lichens with a leaflike structure.

fruiting body — the reproductive structure of a fungus.

fruticose lichens — lichens that form bunches of branches.

gametangium (plural **gametangia**) — a structure that produces gametes.

gamete — a male or female reproductive cell.

genus — a group of rather closely related organisms.

germination — sprouting; the beginning of growth and development of a spore or seed.

gills — thin partitions on the underside of a mushroom cap, in which spores are formed.

Gymnomycota — the subkingdom of slime molds.

hyphae (singular **hypha**) — the threadlike filaments that form the body of a fungus.

kingdom — the largest group in the classification of living organisms.

lichen — a symbiotic association of an alga and a fungus.

mushroom — a gill fungus; a fruiting body of a club fungus consisting of a stem and a cap (which is often umbrella shaped); spores are released from gills on the underside of the cap.

mycelium — the mat or web formed by fungus hyphae.

mycologist — a scientist who studies fungi.

mycology — the study of fungi.

Mycophycota — lichens; a phylum including associations of fungi and algae.

mycorrhiza — a symbiotic association of a fungus and a plant.

Myxomycota — the fungus phylum of acellular slime molds.

Oomycota — a fungus phylum including water molds, downy mildew, and potato blight.

oospore — the product of the joining of an egg and a sperm in water molds.

order — a category in the classification of living organisms (the next smaller after class).

parasite — an organism that lives on or in another organism, taking its nourishment from its host's body.

penicillin — an antibiotic produced by the fungus *Penicillium notatum*.

phylum — a major category in the classification of living organisms.

pore fungi — club fungi whose spores are released from pores rather than gills.

Protista — a kingdom of mainly single-celled organisms.

puffball mushrooms — club fungi with globe-shaped fruiting bodies; spores are released from pores.

rhizomorph — thick, rootlike structures formed by some fungi.

saprophyte — an organism that lives on decaying matter.

sexual reproduction — a form of reproduction in which two parents of different sexes produce offspring that have some of the traits of each parent.

smuts — club fungi that produce enormous numbers of black spores.

species — a group of very closely related organisms, each able to breed with others in the group.

sperm — a male reproductive cell.

sporangium (plural **sporangia**) — spore case; a reproductive structure of slime molds.

spore — a seedlike reproductive cell of fungi.

symbiosis — a relationship in which two organisms of different species live or work together, especially one in which both partners benefit.

taxonomy — the science of classifying or arranging living things into groups based on the characteristics they share.

toadstool — popular name for a poisonous mushroom.

yeast — single-celled sac fungi.

zoospore — a reproductive cell of chytrids, with a flagellum, similar to animal-like protists.

Zygomycota — yoke fungi; a fungus phylum including bread mold, dung fungi, and predatory fungi.

zygospores — thick-walled spores that develop from a zygote in black molds.

zygote — the first cell of a new organism produced by sexual reproduction; the product of the joining of a sperm and an egg.

INDEX

****